Amazing Animal Defenses

Animal Body-Part
Regenerators
Growing New Heads, Tails, and Legs

Susan K. Mitchell

Enslow Publishers, Inc.
40 Industrial Road
Box 398
Berkeley Heights, NJ 07922
USA

http://www.enslow.com

These books are dedicated to Emily, who inspired the author.

Library of Congress Cataloging-in-Publication Data
Mitchell, Susan K.
  Animal body-part regenerators : growing new heads, tails, and legs / by Susan K. Mitchell.
      p. cm. — (Amazing animal defenses)
  Includes bibliographical references.
  Summary: "Readers will learn about animals that can re-grow parts of their bodies, such as tails and legs"—Provided by publisher.
  ISBN 978-0-7660-3295-8
  1. Regeneration (Biology)—Juvenile literature. I. Title.
  QP90.2.M58 2009
  571.8'891—dc22

                          2008011453

ISBN-10: 0-7660-3295-7

Printed in the United States of America
042010 Lake Book Manufacturing, Inc., Melrose Park, IL

10 9 8 7 6 5 4 3 2

To Our Readers:
We have done our best to make sure all Internet Addresses in this book were active and appropriate when we went to press. However, the author and the publisher have no control over and assume no liability for the material available on those Internet sites or on other Web sites they may link to. Any comments or suggestions can be sent by e-mail to comments@enslow.com or to the address on the back cover.

♻ Enslow Publishers, Inc., is committed to printing our books on recycled paper. The paper in every book contains 10% to 30% post-consumer waste (PCW). The cover board on the outside of each book contains 100% PCW. Our goal is to do our part to help young people and the environment too!

Cover photo: airmaria/Fotolia
Interior photos: Alamy/Duncan Usher, p. 4; Alamy/PHOTOTAKE Inc., p. 13; Alamy/WILDLIFE GmbH, p. 15; Alamy/Arco Images GmbH, p. 17; Alamy/David Fleetham, p. 21; Alamy/Tom Mackie, p. 23; Alamy/blickwinkel, p. 25; Alamy/Brandon Cole Marine Photography, p. 26; Alamy/Wolfgang Pölzer, p. 32; Alamy/Stefan Sollfors, p. 33; Alamy/67photo, p. 35; Alamy/Holt Studios International Ltd., p. 36; Alamy/Jenny Matthews, p. 43; Alamy/Neil Cooper, p. 44 (top); Alamy/Penny Tweedie, p. 44 (bottom); Animals Animals–Earth Scenes/J.A.L. Cooke/OSF, p. 40; Corbis/Arthur Morris, p. 28; Fotolia/airmaria, p. 1; iStockphoto/Chartchai Meesangnin, p. 7; iStockphoto/Andrey Prokhorov, p. 8; iStockphoto/David Coder, p. 10; iStockphoto/Paul Morton, p. 18; iStockphoto/Nick Free, p. 27; iStockphoto/Andrei Nekrassov, p. 31; iStockphoto/Tadej Zupancic, p. 38; Oceanwidelmages.com/Gary Bell, p. 22; Photo Researchers, Inc./Joseph T. Collins, p. 12; Photo Researchers, Inc./Mark Boulton, p. 20 (left); Photo Researchers, Inc./Thomas & Pat Leeson, p. 20 (right).

Contents

Chapter 1 Life or Limbs 4

Chapter 2 Growing Super Powers 10

Chapter 3 Marine Magic 18

Chapter 4 Past the Breaking Point 28

Chapter 5 Heads or Tails? 36

Defense Academy for Humans 43

Glossary 45

Further Reading & Internet Addresses 47

Index 48

Life or Limbs

Danger strikes! A predator grabs an animal. It holds tight to the animal's leg or tail. This usually means death for the prey. For a few animals, however, there may still be a chance. Some animals can wrestle free and leave their leg or other body part behind. And for a few other animals, this does not mean they have to live the rest of their lives without a leg or tail. These animals can grow new ones! They are called regenerators.

Some animals can regenerate, or grow back, lost body parts. This lizard's tail is growing back.

Regeneration is an amazing ability. It means that an animal can grow back a lost body part. Very few animals can do this. Some can grow back only a new tail or leg. Others can do a little bit more. They can grow back new eyes or organs. There is even a small group of animals that can grow whole new bodies!

Scientists are not completely sure how the process works. What they do know is that regeneration happens because of changes in an animal's cells. Cells are the smallest basic building block of every living thing. There are many kinds of cells. Some cells make up skin. Others form bone or muscle. There are special cells in nerves and blood. Each kind of cell has a different job in an animal's body.

A regenerator's cells are special. These cells can change jobs. The different cells in the spot where a leg or tail is lost, for example, stop doing their own special jobs. Instead, cells that

5

had different jobs all start doing the same thing. They all help to re-grow the missing body part.

Show a Little Backbone

Almost all animals that can grow new body parts are invertebrates. That means they do not have backbones, or spines. More than 95 percent of the animals in the world have no spine. They also do not have a skeleton inside their bodies. Instead, some of them wear a hard outer skin called an exoskeleton that completely covers their bodies. Others simply have soft bodies or thick shells that partly cover them.

Insects, worms, and spiders are all invertebrates. Animals such as clams, starfish, and crabs also have no backbone. Many animals in this group have very simple bodies. It is easy to forget that they are even animals! Sponges are a good example.

Animals that do have skeletons and backbones are called vertebrates. All birds and mammals have backbones. Reptiles such

The earthworm is an invertebrate. These animals are much better regenerators than vertebrates. They have simpler bodies.

as snakes and lizards also belong to this group. So do frogs and their relatives. Although vertebrates have some power of regeneration, very few can grow new body parts.

That Takes a Lot of Nerve

Animals with backbones usually also have complex nervous systems. The nervous system controls the body. It usually includes a brain and spinal cord. It also has a huge network of nerves. This system controls everything

7

Small Steps for Mankind

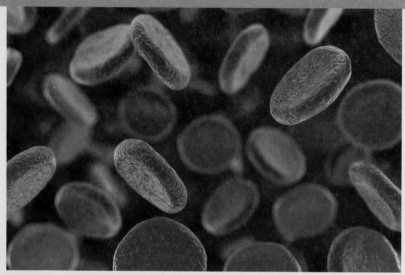

Mammals are not able to grow new body parts. Since humans are mammals, that is true for us, too. If a human loses an arm or leg, it is gone for good. It may heal, but it will never grow back.

Humans can regenerate some things, though. For example, new skin can grow to heal a wound. Bones can grow back together after breaking. New blood cells (above) are made to replace lost blood.

The human liver has amazing regenerating ability. The liver is an organ in the digestive system. It does many important things. If it is damaged, doctors may remove part of it. The part of the liver that is left will grow. It is one of the only parts of the human body with this power.

the body does, from movement to breathing. It controls muscles. It also allows animals to feel temperature and pain.

Most invertebrates also have nervous systems. They are much simpler, however. They do not usually have very advanced brains. Some animals, such as the sponge, have no brain at all. They also do not have a spinal cord. They do have a simple network of nerves. That means that most invertebrates can also feel pain.

Losing a leg, tail, or other body part can really hurt. Most animals will use many other defenses before they leave a leg behind. But when there is a serious threat, it is a small price to pay to escape a predator.

Wild FACT

The hero shrew has the strongest backbone of any animal. It is so strong that this small animal can hold about 160 pounds on its back without being crushed. The hero shrew only weighs about 3 ounces. That is less than one-quarter of a pound. It would be like an average 50-pound kid holding up two school buses!

Chapter 2

Growing Super Powers

Salamanders and newts are survivors. They have many different defenses. Some have camouflage to blend in and hide. They also might try to act or look big to scare off a predator. Others have poisons in their skin. No defense is perfect, however. Salamanders

The red eft (a young newt) has poisonous skin, but it can still be caught by a predator. Luckily it can regenerate a lost tail or leg.

and newts often get caught by other animals. Fortunately, they can also survive the loss of a tail or leg. That is because they have super regenerating powers.

Salamanders and newts are amphibians. Another animal in that group is frogs. These animals all begin life in the water. They also go through some very different stages in their life cycle. Salamanders and newts start out as a small, gooey egg. After hatching, they enter a larval stage. They look nothing like adult salamanders or newts. They are small blobs with a tail but no legs.

Scientists do not fully understand why, but it is during this larval stage when salamanders

 WILD FACT A newt is a kind of salamander, but there are some differences. Generally, newts have rougher skin than salamanders. They also return to water as adults, while salamanders stay on land for the rest of their lives.

Losing By a Tail

Getting caught by a predator is never a good thing. But if a lizard gets caught by the tail, at least it has a chance of surviving. That is because a lizard can lose its tail without serious damage.

There are limits to lizard regeneration, however. Some lizards can grow back only a small bit of the lost tail. Others may be able to grow it back only once. But the fact that a lizard can lose its tail is actually more important than the ability to grow it back. While a predator is busy with a wiggling lizard tail, the lizard can run to safety!

and newts have the best regenerating power. At this stage in life, they are able to grow back body parts quicker and more easily than they can as adults. But even as adults, they still have some ability to regenerate.

It is easier for salamanders to grow back a lost tail when they are in the larval stage.

Getting a Leg Up

While they are living in the water, the biggest threats to salamander and newt larvae are fish. Once on land, the adults find many new predators. Birds and snakes love to eat salamanders and newts. Some mammals eat them, and even other amphibians like frogs eat them. Most of the time salamanders and newts stay hidden under rocks and leaves, away from predators.

Both newts and salamanders are predators also. They are carnivores. That means they eat other animals. Their favorite foods include worms and insects. Eventually newts and salamanders have to come out of hiding to hunt for food. It is then that they are in the most danger.

While out hunting, a newt or salamander is mostly unprotected. It could easily be caught by another animal. Like most animals, the newt or salamander tries very hard to protect its head. If a predator catches its prey by the head or neck, the prey will most likely not survive. On the other hand, if a predator grabs a newt or salamander by the tail or legs, there is still hope for escape.

Losing a leg might be a disaster for some animals. But salamanders and newts can start to repair their missing leg very quickly. In less than 12 hours, a new leg begins to grow and replace the missing one.

Growing Out of Growing Back

Frogs also have some power to grow new body parts, but only when they are tadpoles. A tadpole is a frog's larval form and looks nothing like a frog. It is a legless, black blob with a tail. As the tadpole grows, legs start to sprout and the tail starts to shrink (below). If a predator breaks off the tadpole's tail or leg, the tadpole can grow another to replace it.

Once a tadpole has grown into an adult frog, it loses the ability to regenerate lost body parts. If an adult frog loses its leg, it will not grow back.

Life in a Lab

The secret to the newt's and salamander's regeneration is in their cells. The cells can take over the jobs of other cells. This allows the newt or salamander to grow new skin. It also means that they can grow new muscle and bone. The cells begin to grow and divide. Two cells split and become four, and so on. Soon, there are enough cells to create a new body part.

In most animals with a backbone, any body part that grows back will not be the same as the first one. Arms, legs, or tails may not be as big or as long. The salamander and newt, however, can grow an exact copy of the original

Wild FACT

One of the most popular salamanders used for research is the axolotl (AK-sa-lot-el). This salamander is found in central Mexico. It is not only able to regenerate a lost tail or legs, it can regrow parts of its heart. It can grow new jaws. It can even grow new lenses for its eyes. Most amazing is its ability to regrow parts of its spinal cord!

The axolotl can regenerate almost any part of its body. By studying it, scientists hope to someday help humans who have lost body parts.

limb. At first glance, no one would ever know the part had ever been missing. The new limb looks and works just as good as the limb that was lost.

Scientists still do not know how newts and salamanders can do this. To learn more, scientists study these animals in a research lab. By watching the salamanders repair new legs, tails, and even eyes, they hope to figure out exactly how it is done. Salamanders and newts may one day hold the key to helping scientists learn how to help humans who have lost limbs.

Chapter 3   Marine Magic

Did you know that clones can be found naturally in the animal world? Talk about a real double-take! A clone is an exact copy of a living thing. It is grown and created from the cells of an animal or plant. It sounds weird, but for some animals it is the perfect defense. Starfish are a great example. They are the masters of regeneration. Through regeneration, they can make an exact copy of themselves.

Starfish come in many colors, sizes, and even shapes. They can regenerate just one arm, or a whole new body!

Starfish belong to a group of animals called echinoderms (a-KINE-a-derms). That word means spiny-skinned. While most starfish do not have large spines or spikes, they do have rough or bumpy skin.

Starfish may be beautiful to look at, but they can have a tough life. As adults, they crawl along the ocean floor slowly, looking for any bit of food they can eat. They can easily be seen by predators, but a starfish's tough body wall keeps most animals away. They are not easy to eat.

But there are some ocean animals that do like to eat starfish. Sharks and rays are starfish predators. Some snails and shrimp also eat starfish. The biggest threats to starfish, however, are other, larger starfish!

There are more than 1,000 kinds of starfish, in every size and color. Starfish live in most of the oceans in the world. They can live in warm, tropical seas and in icy, cold polar oceans. They can live in shallow tide pools or on deep, dark ocean floors. Starfish can live just about anywhere.

All starfish have a star-shaped body. Most are easy to spot by this five-armed star shape. But some starfish do not stick to the five-arm rule. The sunflower starfish can have as many as 24 arms. The cushion starfish simply looks like a pentagon (a five-sided shape) with no arms at all. No matter the number, a starfish's arms are the most important thing about its body.

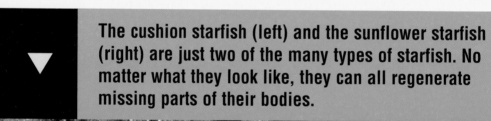

The cushion starfish (left) and the sunflower starfish (right) are just two of the many types of starfish. No matter what they look like, they can all regenerate missing parts of their bodies.

Armed But Not Dangerous

A starfish's arms help it do many things. They help the starfish move from place to place. They also help it eat. Underneath the arms are tiny tube feet. Tube feet look like very small tentacles. There can be hundreds of tube feet under each starfish arm.

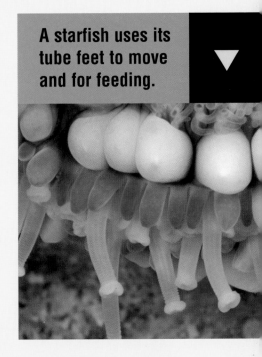

A starfish uses its tube feet to move and for feeding.

The starfish controls its tube feet with small muscles. To move, water from inside the starfish's body is forced through the tube feet. This helps push the starfish along the ocean floor. But a starfish cannot move fast. Starfish move so slowly it sometimes looks like they are not moving at all.

To eat, a starfish uses the small suction cups at the end of each of their tube feet. These give the starfish an amazingly strong grip.

That Takes Guts!

Like starfish, sea cucumbers are also echinoderms. They, too, use tube feet to move. But sea cucumbers look very different from other echinoderms. They have long, thick bodies. Sea cucumbers look more like a lump on the bottom of the ocean than an animal.

Sea cucumbers have a very strange way to escape predators. They can push some of their organs out of their bodies! While a predator is distracted by the sea cucumber's guts floating freely in the water, the sea cucumber has a chance to get away. Losing their insides would kill most animals. A sea cucumber, however, can survive. Not only will it keep living, it can regenerate the lost organs.

A starfish can use its tube feet to pry open and eat shelled animals such as mussels.

Starfish can easily pull open a clam or other shelled animal. They also use their tube feet to bring food to their mouth.

Starfish may look like they are all arms, but they do have a body. The center part of a starfish is its body. It is called a central disk, and is usually divided into five sections. Each section usually has an arm attached.

WILDFACT The crown of thorns starfish can also have more than five arms. Some years there are huge numbers of crown of thorns starfish. These very poisonous starfish eat coral and can completely destroy a coral reef.

The center part of a starfish is where its two stomachs are located. The mouth is located underneath. A starfish does not have a heart or brain. Instead, it has a nerve ring around the mouth area. Simple nerves branch off the ring to each arm.

Wild FACT A starfish uses its arms to push food into its mouth. Some starfish can push their stomachs outside of their mouths to eat!

Gimme Five!

Most of a starfish's major organs are inside its arms. For example, each arm has reproductive organs. Each arm also has pouches that come off of the main stomach. If a starfish is caught by a predator, it can simply lose its arm. The predator is usually too busy with the arm to notice that the rest of the starfish has gotten away.

Starfish arms are made to break off very easily. Losing an arm is very common for

24

Losing an arm is not a big deal for a starfish. This starfish's missing arm is just starting to grow back.

starfish. Since they can grow new ones, it is not a big loss. If a starfish loses an arm without also losing part of the central disk, it will grow another arm. The new arm is often smaller than the original arm. But it still works like the old one, and the starfish will survive. What happens to the broken-off arm? Sometimes, the arm might not be eaten by the predator. It might simply fall to the ocean floor.

25

On the other hand, if a lost arm includes part of the central disk, the arm itself can also regenerate. The damaged arm will begin to grow four more arms. Soon, there is a completely new starfish from just one arm! By losing its arm, not only will the original starfish live through an attack, but a whole new one might be created.

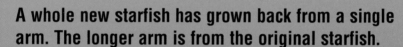

A whole new starfish has grown back from a single arm. The longer arm is from the original starfish.

The Simple Life

Animals do not get much simpler than a sponge. Sponges have no true organs. They are not much more than a group of living cells. They come in many shapes, sizes, and colors. One thing all sponges have in common are their pores. Pores are the holes all over a sponge's body.

These holes let water pass through the sponge. Food is filtered from the water. Sponges cannot move, so they simply sit and wait for food. This means that they cannot get away from predators. But having such a simple body makes regeneration easy for a sponge. It can grow back any part of its body that might get eaten.

Chapter 4

Past the Breaking Point

Crayfish go by many names. They are called crawfish, crawdads, or mud bugs. Whatever they are called, one thing stays the same. Although crayfish have a great ability to regenerate, their ability has limits. They can only grow new legs. If any other body part gets lost, a crayfish is out of luck.

What makes a crayfish special is that it is one of the few animals that can choose to lose

Some seabirds love to make a meal out of a crayfish. But the crayfish still has a chance to get away. It can lose a leg, which will grow back.

a leg. Most animals that can grow new body parts cannot do that. Their limbs are bitten or ripped off by predators. The crayfish is different. It can make its leg pop off on purpose. That is a handy trick if a predator has hold of a crayfish by the leg.

Crayfish look like tiny lobsters. In fact, they are actually a close cousin of the lobster. Both belong to a group of animals called crustaceans (krus-TAY-shuns). Shrimp also belong to this group. Crayfish are found in the southern United States, as well as in many other places, such as Asia, Europe, and New Zealand.

Most crayfish live in freshwater rivers and streams. Very few crayfish live in saltwater. But crayfish can live in many different areas. Some live in swamps or small ponds. Others are just as happy living in a roadside ditch.

During the day, crayfish spend their time hiding under rocks or logs. They are mostly nocturnal. That means they are active at night. That is when they hunt for food. Crayfish eat insect larvae and small worms or fish. Plants are also on their menu. They will eat just about anything. Eating both plants and animals makes them omnivores.

Wild FACT Many people love to eat crayfish. Farming and raising crayfish is a big business in the southern United States, where they are called crawfish. Each year, more than 100 million pounds of crawfish are farmed in Louisiana alone.

Put Your Right Leg In . . .

A crayfish's body is made of two parts. The front part includes the head and is called the cephalothorax (sef-a-low-THOR-ax). The back end of the crayfish is the abdomen. It is made up of several segments, or sections.

Crayfish belong to a group of animals called crustaceans. These animals have hard outer shells known as exoskeletons.

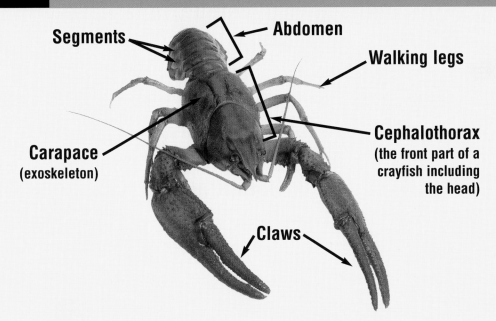

Segments

Abdomen

Walking legs

Cephalothorax
(the front part of a
crayfish including
the head)

Carapace
(exoskeleton)

Claws

Crayfish are partly covered in a very hard outer shell called a carapace (KARE-a-pace). The carapace is also called an exoskeleton. This helps to protect the crayfish's soft body.

The carapace of a crayfish does not grow. So, when the crayfish's body grows it must shed the shell. This is called molting. When a crayfish molts, the hard outer shell splits open. The crayfish crawls out of the too-small shell. During this time, it is in a lot of danger. Its body is soft and unprotected.

After a few days, a new shell hardens and the crayfish is protected again.

The exoskeleton gives the crayfish some safety, but it is not perfect. Many predators have learned to crack the hard outer shell. Others have teeth that can easily bite through the crayfish's shell. A crayfish needs a defensive back-up plan. That is where its legs come in.

The crayfish has four pairs of walking legs. These legs are attached to the cephalothorax. They are long and jointed. On the crayfish's abdomen are five pairs of smaller legs. Although these are not true legs, they do help the crayfish move around.

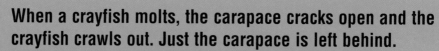

▼ When a crayfish molts, the carapace cracks open and the crayfish crawls out. Just the carapace is left behind.

It's Good to Be Young

Spiders may not seem to have much in common with crayfish, but they are alike in some ways. They both molt. They both have jointed legs that can be regenerated. However, there is one way that spiders are more like frogs than crayfish. They can regenerate lost legs only when they are young.

A baby spider can grow back a lost leg. An adult spider cannot. Like a crayfish, a spider's outer skin does not grow with it. A spider molts as it grows. Since a young spider will molt several times before it becomes an adult, it has many chances to regenerate if it has to.

If a baby spider loses a leg, a new one will grow back. The new leg will get bigger each time the spider molts. When a spider is fully grown, it stops molting. Then the spider can no longer grow back a lost leg (above). Sometimes, a spider may lose a leg and have only one or two more molt cycles left in its life. This means a leg might grow back, but it will not be as large as the other legs.

It's a Snap!

At the top of each leg, the crayfish has a "breaking joint." A joint is the place where body parts meet, such as elbows, knees, and shoulders on a human. Joints allow body parts to move. The breaking joints of a crayfish are found right where the eight walking legs meet the cephalothorax.

Limits on Losing Legs

Like crayfish, many insects and spiders can grow new legs if they lose the old ones. But this works only if they lose one or two legs. If any animal loses too many legs, it can be in danger.

Insects, spiders, and crayfish all use their legs for many reasons. They use them for movement. They can use them for defense. They also use them for getting food. If these animals lose too many legs, they could die before they are able to grow new ones. Without legs that can catch food, they will starve before regeneration is finished.

34

A crayfish's breaking joints are located where the legs meet the body.

All animals that can lose a body part on purpose have this special area that can easily break away when the animal needs to drop a leg or tail. This also helps when the new body part begins to grow back. It helps make sure that the new leg will be the same size and just as strong as the other legs.

Wild FACT A crayfish also has weapons it can use against predators. It has two front legs with large claws. These strong claws can give a very painful pinch! These claw arms also have a breaking joint, and can grow back if they are broken off.

Chapter 5

Heads or Tails?

It is not easy being an earthworm. An earthworm cannot move very fast. It spends most of its time deep in dirt. Earthworms are also a favorite meal of many animals. At first glance, it might seem like earthworms have no way to defend themselves from predators.

An earthworm digs through the soil, eating all the time. What they eat is dirt. That

An earthworm spends its life tunneling through the dirt. This simple animal can lose its tail end and grow a new one to survive.

might not sound very good to a human, but the dirt is full of minerals and other things that are very healthy for the earthworm.

All of this digging and eating make earthworms very important to plant growth. The tunnels earthworms make under the soil let air pass through the soil. The tunnels also help water flow to plant roots. This helps plants grow. The dirt that is digested by the worm helps plants as well.

Into the Underground

The simple, dirt-eating life of an earthworm is far from safe. Hundreds of birds, mammals, reptiles, and amphibians love an earthworm

Wild FACT One of the biggest earthworms in the world is the giant Gippsland earthworm of Australia. It can grow to more than 10 feet long. But the longest earthworm ever found was in South Africa. It was more than 22 feet long!

lunch. The first line of defense for any earthworm is to stay hidden. Living under the ground helps, but only a little.

Earthworms do come to the surface sometimes, usually at night or after it rains. This is because the air and soil are more moist at these times. The earthworm does not have lungs. It breathes through its skin. This means that earthworms must always stay moist. If their skin dries out, they cannot breathe and will die. Underground, earthworms get air from spaces in the loose soil. When it rains, these spaces fill up with water and the earthworm has to come to the surface to breathe.

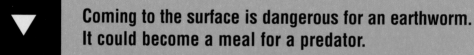

Coming to the surface is dangerous for an earthworm. It could become a meal for a predator.

This is a dangerous trip for an earthworm to make. Coming to the surface means the earthworm is out in the open. It makes it easy pickings for a predator. Staying underground is safer. Even then, however, the earthworm is not completely out of danger. Many mammals dig deep to find earthworms to eat.

The earthworm does have a few tricks to stay safe. First of all, an earthworm is an invertebrate. Without a backbone, the earthworm can twist and wriggle in almost any shape or direction. It can be hard for a predator to get a good grip on a wiggling worm.

Also, an earthworm's body is lined with very tiny hairs called setae (SEE-tee). They are so small that human eyes cannot see them. These tiny hairs help the earthworm move from place to place. They also can act like anchors to keep the worm in one spot. The setae can stick tight against the walls of the worm's tunnel. This can make it harder for a predator to pull an earthworm out of its hole.

An earthworm cannot grow a new head. This earthworm is growing new tail segments.

head segments

new tail segments

Splitting up Is Hard to Do

But sometimes all of a predator's pulling can cause disaster to strike. An earthworm can be pulled apart. Fortunately, the earthworm has a secret defensive weapon. Even if the predator gets a mouthful of the worm's tail, the earthworm might still survive. That is because an earthworm can regenerate most of its body.

An earthworm's body is made up of many segments. These are ring-like body parts. Some earthworms may have as many as 100 body segments, or even more. The front segments of an earthworm hold the important body organs. Inside these segments is a very small, simple brain. There are also five hearts. The front segments are also where the earthworm's major digestive organs are located.

Clearly, an earthworm's front segments are the most important. If the earthworm is split, the front end will grow new tail segments. The cut-off tail segments of the injured worm might also regenerate. The only problem is that this will make a worm with two tail ends instead of one with a head end and a tail end. An earthworm cannot regenerate another head. Eventually the worm with two tail ends will die

Wild FACT In a one-acre area of land, there may be more than a million earthworms under the ground!

of starvation. How an earthworm regenerates all depends on where it is cut in two!

Building Body Parts

Growing new body parts sounds a little like science fiction. But in the animal world, it is very real. Having the ability to live through a predator's attack that could kill another animal gives regenerators a huge advantage. They can escape, heal, grow, and survive.

Like most animals, those that can regenerate body parts try to avoid predator attacks in the first place. However, if they are attacked, the fact that they can lose a body part gives them a chance to get away that most animals never have. Whether it is a leg or tail that can be sacrificed for survival, regeneration is a truly amazing animal defense.

No matter how good human defenses may be, serious injuries do happen. Many weapons are difficult to defend against. Weapons such as land mines and other explosives, for example, may remain hidden. These weapons are made to create maximum destruction. It is very hard to defend against something that cannot be seen until it is too late.

Land mines are made to be buried underground. They are triggered to explode when a person walks near them. Land mines have been used by armed forces for many years.

A major problem with land mines is that they can be hard to find after the fighting is over. When a battle is done and troops have moved on, many land mines may still lie buried under the dirt. They can lie there for years. No one may know a land mine is there until he or she takes one wrong step.

Many parts of the world are affected by land mines. Africa, however, has had more land mine victims than anywhere else. More than half of that continent has unexploded land mines scattered throughout the land. Many people all across Africa are injured every

A worker wears a shield to protect his face as he searches for buried land mines (above). The mines are often small (below) and stay hidden in the ground for years.

year by accidentally stepping on undiscovered land mines. A large number of those victims are children. The injuries are almost always very serious. Many people are killed. The people who live often lose limbs.

Scientists all over the world have spent years studying animals that can regenerate. Many of them study stem cells. These are special cells than can change what they normally do. Scientists hope that by figuring out how stem cells work, they can one day find a way to help humans regenerate limbs. This will help land mine victims all over the world.

Scientists already know many of the ways that animals' cells work. What they have not figured out is if human cells might be able to do the same thing. In this case, regeneration would not be used as a defense. But it could be a key to survival.

Glossary

amphibians—Cold-blooded animals that can live both on land and in water, such as salamanders.

camouflage—When an animal uses its appearance or color to blend in with its surroundings.

carapace—A hard, protective shell-like covering of an animal.

carnivores—Animals that eat meat.

cells—The tiny, basic building blocks of all living things.

cephalothorax—The front section of animals such as spiders or crabs. It is made up of the head and thorax.

clones—Exact copies of a living thing.

crustaceans—A class of animals that live in water and have shells.

echinoderms—A group of ocean animals with spiny skins.

exoskeleton—The hard outer covering of some animals that provides protection.

invertebrates—Animals with no backbone.

larval—An early stage in the life of many animals.

45

molting—When an animal sheds its outer covering as it grows.

nervous system—A system of the body that usually includes a brain, spinal cord, and a network of nerves. It controls everything the body does, from movement to breathing.

nocturnal—Being active at night and at rest during the day.

omnivore—An animal that eats both meat and plants.

predator—An animal that hunts and eats other animals.

prey—Any animal that is a food source for other animals.

regeneration—The ability to grow back missing body parts such as tails and legs.

setae—Stiff hairs or bristles.

tentacles—Arm-like body parts of many types of sea animals.

vertebrates—Animals with a backbone.

Further Reading

Books

Dixon, Norma. *Earthworms*. Markham, On.: Fitzhenry & Whiteside, 2005.

Gilpin, Daniel. *Starfish, Urchins & Other Echinoderms*. Mankato, Minn.: Compass Point Books, 2006.

Rhodes, Mary Jo, and David Hall. *Survival Secrets of Sea Animals*. Danbury, Conn.: Children's Press, 2007.

Internet Addresses

Discovery Kids: Worm World
http://yucky.discovery.com/noflash/worm/index.html

National Geographic Kids: Creature Feature—
Spotted Salamanders
http://kids.nationalgeographic.com/Animals/Creature
Feature/Salamander

Newt Limb Regeneration
http://www.luc.edu/faculty/wwasser/dev/regen2.htm

Index

A

amphibians, 11, 13, 37
arms, 8, 16, 20, 21, 23,
  24–26, 35

B

birds, 6, 13, 37
blood, 5, 8
bones, 5, 8, 16
brains, 7, 9, 24, 41

C

cells, 5–6, 8, 16, 18, 27, 44
crayfish, 28–35
crustaceans, 29

E

earthworms, 36–42
eyes, 5, 16, 17

F

food, 14, 19, 23, 24, 27, 30, 34
frogs, 7, 11, 13, 15, 33

H

hearts, 16, 24, 41
humans, 8, 17, 34, 43–44

I

insects, 6, 14, 30, 34
invertebrates, 6, 9, 39

L

land mines, 43–44
legs, 4, 5, 8, 9, 11, 14, 15, 16,
  17, 28–29, 32, 33, 34, 35, 42
lizards, 7, 12

M

mammals, 6, 8, 13, 37, 39
muscles, 5, 9, 16, 21

N

nerves/nervous systems, 5,
  7, 9, 16, 24
newts, 10–11, 13–14, 16–17

O

organs, 5, 8, 22, 24, 27, 41

P

predators, 4, 9, 10, 12, 13, 14,
  15, 19, 22, 24, 25, 27, 29,
  32, 35, 36, 39, 40, 42

R

reptiles, 6–7, 37

S

salamanders, 10–11, 13–14,
  16–17
sea cucumbers, 22
shells, 6, 31–32
skin, 5, 6, 8, 10, 11, 16, 19,
  33, 38
spiders, 6, 33, 34
sponges, 6, 9, 27
starfish, 6, 18–21, 23–26

T

tails, 4, 5, 9, 11, 12, 14, 15, 16,
  17, 35, 40, 41, 42
tube feet, 21, 22, 23

V

vertebrates, 6–7